To De[...]

"Merry Christmas"
1991
lots of love
Lizbeth xxx.

OLD DUNDEE

Old Dundee

PICTURE POSTCARDS

Andrew Cronshaw

MAINSTREAM
PUBLISHING

First published in Great Britain in 1988 by
MAINSTREAM PUBLISHING CO. (EDINBURGH) LTD.
7 Albany Street
Edinburgh EH1 3UG

ISBN 1 85158 184 7 (cloth)

British Library Cataloguing in Publication Data
Cronshaw, Andrew
    Old Dundee picture postcards.
    1. Scotland. Tayside region. Dundee. —
    History
    941.2'7

    ISBN 1-85158-184-7

Typeset in Goudy by Polyprint, 48 Pleasance, Edinburgh EH8 9TJ.
Colour Separations by Creative Colour Repro, Glasgow.
Design by Paul Keir.
Printed and bound by Richard Clays, Bungay.

To My Parents

ACKNOWLEDGEMENTS

All postcards were selected from the author's collection except for the plates now mentioned.

Dundee Art Galleries and Museums
Page 124   TOP

Dundee Central Library
Page   45   TOP RIGHT
Page   45   BOTTOM RIGHT
Page   56   TOP
Page   83   TOP RIGHT
Page 105   TOP RIGHT
Page 105   BOTTOM RIGHT
Page 123   TOP RIGHT

The Valentine Collection, St Andrews University
Page   15
Page   57   BOTTOM RIGHT
Page   58   TOP
Page 109   TOP RIGHT

Apologies for any inadvertent omission in attribution.

FOREWORD

Several years ago I organised an exhibition of picture postcards in one of Glasgow's many fine art galleries and museums. It revealed to me two things — first, the importance of the picture postcard as a historical record, and second, the awakening of public interest in old cards.

This book presents many facets of Dundee, one of the birthplaces of picture postcards, and contributes to historical records of the city. In an age of rapid change, postcards still have an appeal and a relevance to the theme, "This was and is Dundee".

James D. Boyd, O.B.E., D.A., F.M.A.,
Director of Art Galleries and Museums,
Dundee, 1949-1982.

INTRODUCTION

Dundee today is being energetically promoted as the "City of Discovery". This book attempts to discover the city as it was in Victorian and Edwardian times and onwards until the early 1930s. Particular emphasis has been placed on scenes which have changed, buildings that have been demolished, traditional industries that have disappeared and the people who shaped the city. Whilst some redevelopment of the outmoded Victorian structures was to be expected, many people regret that so much of our heritage has been lost.

Early industries in Dundee included soap manufacture, window glass and bottle making, and sugar refining. A reminder of these industries remains today in the street names "Soap Work Lane" and "Sugar House Wynd". In the early 18th century Dundee's main industry was the spinning and weaving of coarse woollen plaiding. By the end of the 18th century spinning and weaving of flax became more important. Cotton and coloured thread were also manufactured in the city at this time. In the 1750s Dundee began to develop as a whaling centre. However, by the turn of the century there was a slump in this industry. This was revived in the second half of the 19th century when it was found that whale oil could be used as a lubricant in one of the spinning processes in the growing jute industry. Flax had been primarily imported from Russia. During the Crimean War, in the middle of the 19th century, this raw material was difficult to obtain and expensive. Jute was a suitable replacement. It was cheap, readily available and new techniques of manufacture meant that it had a bright future which was exploited. The flax and jute industry gave employment to most people in Dundee. The town grew out of all recognition. The population of just over 45,000 in 1831 had reached almost 79,000 in 1851. By 1871 it had increased to over 120,000 and 20 years later was almost 156,000. By 1872, 72 jute mills and factories in the city employed 42,000 people. This represented about one in three of the total population. By the 1860s and 1870s Dundee had developed as the world centre of the jute trade. However, the periods of prosperity and growth gave no indication of the harder times that lay ahead. As early as 1855 the first jute mill had been built in India. India was Dundee's greatest competitor with unlimited cheap labour. The boom years of the 1860s and 1870s were followed by decline in demand and over capacity. By 1900 India had captured much of the world jute trade.

Shipbuilding was an important industry in Dundee. The *Discovery* was built by Dundee Shipbuilders Co. Ltd in 1901. They were the successor of the firm of Alexander Stephen & Sons. The founder, Alexander Stephen (1795-1875), moved to Dundee with his four sons in 1844 where they occupied the Panmure Yard at Marine Parade. William Stephen with his father ran the Dundee firm while two of his brothers started a firm of shipbuilders in Glasgow. Many orders were placed with the Dundee firm for whaling vessels. When iron-shipbuilding was introduced the firm took it up at once. On the death of William Stephen in September 1893 the Dundee yard closed and the firm concentrated on the Clyde. The business of the yard was taken up in 1895 by Dundee Shipbuilders Co. Ltd. In 1912 the firm became the Dundee Shipbuilding Co. Ltd. In addition, smaller numbers were engaged in iron-foundries, light engineering, flour mills, confectionery manufacture and publishing as these businesses developed.

Austria-Hungary issued the first plain postcard on 1 October 1869. Exactly one year later the first British postcard was issued by the Post Office. Its monopoly prevented picture postcard development until 1894 when privately printed postcards for use with adhesive stamps were permitted. The first British view cards were produced in September 1894 by George Stewart & Co., Edinburgh. George Stewart was born in Dundee in 1834 and had worked in James Chalmers bookshop, in Castle Street, before he started his own business as a manufacturing stationer in Edinburgh in 1879. Until 1897 no message was allowed on the address side, the picture on the front was reduced in size to leave space for the message. In 1902 the "divided back" card was introduced in Britain which allowed the message and address to be written on the same side. The heyday of the picture postcard in Britain, which developed into a collecting craze, was between 1895 and 1915. By 1903 some 600 million cards were sent annually. This peaked at 880 million in 1914. On 3 June 1918 the price of sending a postcard doubled to 1d. In the year that followed half the previous year's number of postcards were sent. The cards, mostly costing 1d. each, occupied the role of the telephone today. Local deliveries were frequent. It was common to have at least four collections a day with guaranteed same-day delivery within a local area. Pictures and photographs were rare in newspapers. This provided an attraction to the sender, especially if their street, house or they themselves appeared on the card. One of the interests of old postcards today are their messages which reflect aspects of the period in which they were sent. Writing home to Folkestone, Kent, in 1909, a lady described her journey and first impressions of Dundee to her sister: "We arrived safe over the Tay Bridge. It was dark and we started at 2 o'clock Sunday morning and arrived at 10.30 just as all the people were going to church. It was a sight in all their kilts. What a large place this is, just like London."

Not all impressions of the city were favourable. One correspondent remarked: "There are some wide streets in Dundee but all stone — They say in marmalade time the smell from Keiller's factories is dreadful." Keiller's factory was situated in the centre of Dundee. All around the city were numerous factory chimneys which poured out dirty smoke. The resulting air pollution should not be overlooked in any nostalgic retrospective on our industrial cities. It was not until 1958 that the Clean Air Act came into force and banned black smoke.

One of Britain's largest producers of postcards, on a vast scale, was James Valentine & Sons Ltd, at their Westfield Works, Perth Road, Dundee. Many photographs of Dundee were taken by Valentines in 1903. These appear as mass produced and often poorly printed postcards. As techniques for postcard production improved, real photograph postcards were introduced. Valentines were producing such cards around 1907, although some of the London publishing firms specialised in this type of card and were initially ahead of Valentines in this technique. The original photographs used showed no clouds. The emulsions used at this time were slow and mainly sensitive to violet and blue light, so that the exposure time needed for the rest of the picture resulted in the sky being overexposed. After development the sky came out unnaturally clear. This is shown in the photographic cards, but the clouds could be retouched by artists when the picture was to be lithographically printed. By 1914 Valentines could produce very high quality photographic cards quickly. The postcards of the Royal Visit to Dundee on 10 July 1914 went on sale at 7.30 p.m. that day, just five and a half hours after the Royal Party had left. Valentines produced their last monochrome postcards in 1967 and last colour postcards in 1970. Today the firm continues to produce Christmas and greetings cards.

It is important to note that the dates given in this book refer to the date when the photographs were taken and not when the cards were issued. Postcards of the Tay Bridge Disaster could not be produced in 1879 but were issued some 30 years later. Certain pictures would be used for several years and then updated. Others, where the view had not changed, would be kept in production for several decades. An example of a small local publisher was that of Cynicus Publishing Co. Ltd, Tayport, Fife. "Cynicus" was the pseudonym of artist Martin Anderson. He was born in 1854 at Leuchars, Fife, and issued his first postcard in 1902. The firm survived until 1916. Another local publisher, based in Dundee, was J. B. White of the Cowgate. He produced many local postcards but never on the scale of Valentines.

Local photographers also produced postcards of the locality and special events to sell in their shops. An example would be George Petrie of Main Street, Dundee.

Looking at the varied street scenes in these postcards, it is evident that Dundee was full of local characters, and a fascinating assortment of signs advertising all kinds of goods and services. There were many family businesses. Amongst the prominent businessmen was David Tulloch, who founded the firm of H. and W. Tulloch, the hatters, around 1820. Originally there were three shops, one in the High Street, one in the Murraygate and another in the Wellgate. David died in 1849 and for the next 15 years the shops were managed by his widow. On the death of their mother, Henry and William partnered the business. In the early 1880s they discarded the old premises and moved to the corner of Reform Street. In 1896 William died and eight years later Henry died. The business continued until 1909 when the site was bought by H. Samuel the jewellers.

A number of local businessmen rose to the position of Lord Provost. One such person was Sir James Low. He came to Dundee from Kirriemuir and in 1868 opened up his first grocer's shop in Hunter Street. In 1871 he entered in to partnership with William Lindsay, the firm prospered and survives today in the firm of William Low & Co. Another successful business was G. L. Wilson's drapery store at 2 Murraygate. In 1903, Gavin Laurie's son, Garnet Wilson, joined the family business. He later became manager of the store and Dundee's Lord Provost during the Second World War. He closed his store for the last time on 31 December 1971.

In 1908 Winston Churchill, a radical liberal, who sought social improvement for local people, became M.P. for Dundee. It was described to him as a comfortable "seat for life". However, in the General Election of 16 November 1922, Edwin Scrymgeour ousted Churchill to become the first and only Prohibitionist M.P. Churchill's defeat was a sensational loss in an election in which 81 per cent of the electorate voted. The Scottish Temperance Movement began in the early 19th century when drunkenness was recognised as a serious problem in the country. The movement was very strong and closely linked with radical politics. Scrymgeour held his seat until 1931.

The postcards show that over the years Dundee hosted a number of Royal Visits. On 11 September 1844 Queen Victoria, Prince Albert and the Princess Royal landed in the city on their way to the Highlands and Blair Atholl. They passed under the triumphal arch at the north end of Mid Quay and toured through the brightly decorated streets. Queen Victoria passed through the city again in June 1879 when she crossed the Tay by the first and ill-fated Tay Bridge to confer a knighthood on Thomas Bouch, its designer. The third and last occasion of her passing through Dundee was in June 1891 when she crossed the new Tay Bridge. Queen Alexandra and Princess Victoria departed for Norway from Dundee in August 1907 and 1908. King George V, Queen Mary and Princess Mary visited Dundee on 10 July 1914. They were taken from the station by Royal carriage to the Albert Institute where the King inspected a Guard of Honour. Moving on, the King, Queen and Princess were presented to William Boyd, managing director of James Keiller & Sons. Janet Keiller (1737-1813) and her son James founded the firm in 1797 after inadvertently discovering how to make marmalade from a consignment of Seville oranges. A high point on the tour was a visit to Ashton Works, Hawkhill, where Sir James Caird showed the Royal Party around the mill. Before leaving Ashton Works the Royal visitors formally laid the foundation stone for the new Town Hall, donated to the city by Sir James Caird. This was achieved by the King and Queen each pressing an electric button, causing two stones, suspended from two carefully balanced beams, to be slowly lowered into place in the Greenmarket. They then left Ashton Works for a visit to Baxter Bros. Dens Works. On their way the first and most dramatic suffragette incident occurred. The suffragette headquarters in Dundee was known to be in a one-storey building, in the Nethergate, which had a flat roof and was on the Royal route. The police anticipated possible trouble, so before the procession started, detectives climbed up ladders onto the flat roof. Looking through the skylight they saw Miss Olive Watson, Organising Secretary, about to climb a ladder. The detectives, smiling, nailed down the skylight. The lady ran out of the front door to be "shadowed" by another detective. She ran to Victoria Road, near Hilltown. Just as the Royal carriage passed she rushed out from the crowd and threw what was thought to be a bomb into the carriage. A rubber ball with a suffragette petition attached to it landed at the Queen's feet. Miss Watson was removed by two officers and taken to the Central Police Station. The rest of the tour passed off successfully.

Having laid the foundation stone for the Caird Hall during this visit, members of the Royal family returned to open the hall on its completion. H.R.H. Prince Edward performed this duty in 1923, followed by H.R.H. Prince George ten years later, who opened the City Chambers. Her Majesty Queen Elizabeth, when she was Princess Elizabeth, opened Camperdown Park to the public on

28 September 1948. In 1961 the Queen Mother opened the Arts Tower and Library of Queen's College, and on 1 August 1967 Queen's College became the University of Dundee and the Queen Mother became the first Chancellor.

I would like to thank the following people for their invaluable assistance and support which enabled me to prepare this book: Adam B. Ritchie, Curator; Janice Murray, Keeper of Human History; and Nancy Davey, Schools Officer; at Dundee Art Galleries and Museums. J. B. Ramage, Chief Librarian; Ruth Riding, Head of Reference Services; and Linda McGill, Local History Librarian; at Dundee Central Library. Joan Auld, University Archivist; and Michael Shafe, Deputy Librarian at Dundee University Library. Iain Flett, City Archivist. Karen Cunningham, Special Collections Library Assistant, at Aberdeen University Library. Robert N. Smart, Keeper of Manuscripts, at St Andrews University Library.

For their apt comments and suggestions I thank Maureen and Veronica Boath; Dr G. D. Brindle; Alan Brotchie; Alan Constable; Howard Davis; Bill Early; Thomas Flood; Wilfred Grubb; Stewart Harris; Jack Herd; C. W. Hill; Andrew Johnstone; Charlotte Lythe; W. J. MacGregor; James Mair; Charles McKean; Douglas Mucklow; R. Nimmo; Rev. Ian Petrie; John Rundle; T. C. Smout; Douglas Spence; Silvie Taylor; Neil Thomas; David Walker; Forbes Walker; Robin Whalley and Firemaster Alex Winston. Thanks are extended to Linda McGill for reading the manuscript and to D. Caldeira for typing the text.

Andrew Cronshaw
Edinburgh
June 1988

JAMES VALENTINE, 1815-1879

James Valentine was the true founder of Valentine & Sons, Dundee, one of the most prominent and prolific postcard publishers. The firm evolved from a business started by his father, John Valentine (1792-1868). John worked as a linen manufacturer in Dundee until 1825. He then changed career and became an engraver of wood blocks used for printing linen. By 1832 James had qualified as a portrait painter and joined the family business. He introduced steel engraving as a replacement for the wood blocks. In the 1840s John emigrated to America. James kept apace with the new techniques of photography which were developing during this period. In the early 1850s he went to Paris to study photography. He returned to Dundee and by 1856 had established himself as a photographer at 100 Murraygate. In 1858 his business moved to 23 High street. At this time he was involved in engravings, lithographic printing, bookbinding, and picture-framing, as well as photography. In 1863 James' eldest son William entered the firm. He specialised in landscape photography, while his brother, George, concentrated on portrait work. When James died in 1879 his two sons became partners. Around 1886 William was left in sole charge of the firm when George departed due to ill health. In 1896 the firm became a limited company. Valentines produced their first court-size postcards c 1897.

E 03095

TAY BRIDGE, DUNDEE, (FROM THE SOUTH)

ABOVE: WORMIT STATION circa 1914
The railway from Dundee to Newport opened for traffic on 12 May 1879. The station at Wormit, opened ten years later, served commuters from this new village. On 7 August 1897 a train leaving Newport failed to stop at a signal and collided into the platform. Nobody was killed but about 40 feet of platform were completely demolished. The last train from Wormit Station left on 3 May 1969.

TOP RIGHT: CRAIG PIER 1883
Craig Pier and the slipway at Newport were designed by engineer Thomas Telford for a regular new steam ferry service. The first Tay steam ferries were the paddle steamers *Union* and *George IV*, built in 1821 and 1823 by Brown of Perth with engines by James Carmichael & Co. Ltd of Dundee. The paddle steamer shown here is the *Dundee*.

BOTTOM RIGHT: THE TAY FROM NINEWELLS circa 1904
At the end of the 18th century the town was clustered around Market-Gait, now the High Street. During the 19th century the city expanded rapidly with the importance of the whaling industry and development of jute manufacture. By the 20th century Ninewells was at the City Boundary. This card was published by the Cynicus Publishing Co. Ltd., Tayport, Fife.

Tay Ferry Steamers, Dundee

Western Necropolis Entrance. Dundee   Valentines Series

ABOVE: PERTH ROAD 1903
The centre of the picture on the single tack shows tramcar No. 32 which was heading for the High Street from Ninewells or West Park Road. The entrance on the right leads to the Western Cemetery which opened in 1847. James Chalmers (1782-1853), the insufficiently recognised inventor of the postage stamp, was buried here.

TOP RIGHT: PERTH ROAD FROM SINDERINS circa 1908
Blackness Library shown on the right was erected in 1908 for a sum of £7,000 and presented to the citizens of Dundee by Andrew Carnegie LL.D. (1835-1919). Carnegie was born in great poverty in Dunfermline, and emigrated to America where he developed a huge steel "empire". With his profits, he endowed various foundations for educational work.

BOTTOM RIGHT: SINDERINS 1903
This junction was named Sinderins since it refers to the separation of roads. The Hawkhill, leading off to the left, was the main highway from Perth to Dundee until Perth Road was built. The tenements on the left of Hawkhill form Gowrie Place, and have recently been restored. An open-top tram No. 39 was heading along a deserted Perth Road towards Ninewells terminus.

Perth Road from Sinderins, Dundee.

63266.JV.

39121

The Sinderins, Dundee

Valentines Series

NETHERGATE AND CAIRD "REST", DUNDEE

ABOVE: NETHERGATE AND CAIRD REST circa 1914
The Queen's Hotel in the centre was designed in 1878 by Young and Meldrum of Perth as Dundee's equivalent to Edinburgh's North British Hotel. The new West Station was built some ten years later but was situated closer to the town centre. The entrance gates on the left lead to University College. On the right at 172 Nethergate stands the Caird Rest, a place of rest and recreation for elderly citizens, opened in 1912.

TOP RIGHT: NETHERGATE circa 1912
The spire on the right belongs to St Paul's Church. It was designed by George Wilson of Glasgow in the early 1850s. The spires of the Town House and St Paul's Cathedral are seen afar. The shop on the left was 97 Nethergate, belonging to M. Cochrane (modist). At No. 95 was E. J. Scotland (bootmaker), at No. 93 Mrs Scott (corsetmaker) and at No. 91 was surgical instrument maker, Charles Allardyce.

BOTTOM RIGHT: NETHERGATE LOOKING WEST circa 1904
The road leading off to the right was Lindsay Street. It is now a pedestrian area and forms part of the new Overgate. William Lindsay (1767-1849), from whom the street acquired its name, was Provost from 1831-1833. On the corner of Lindsay Street was A. Davie, a dental mechanic, who succeeded Dr Stewart, surgeon and dentist. The twin church tower on the right belonged to St Enoch's Church.

Nethergate looking E., Dundee.

Nethergate looking West, Dundee.

Blackness Avenue, Dundee

ABOVE: BLACKNESS AVENUE *circa 1910*

Blackness Avenue was originally the approach to Blackness House, which was demolished in the late 1920s. Access to Blackness House would have been from the point where Corso Street now meets Blackness Avenue, which was just beyond the most distant tenement shown in the picture. Blackness Library is shown on the left.

TOP RIGHT: PARK TERRACE FROM THE TOP OF SEYMOUR STREET *circa 1914*

This picture of Blackness Road shows a tramcar on part of the Balgay Lodge route. This line ran from High Street to Tay Street to West Port where it became double track to Ure Street. From Ure Street there was single track with passing points which connected up to the terminus at Balgay Lodge. The line was extended from Balgay to Blackness in March 1914.

BOTTOM RIGHT: PERTH ROAD AT MILLER'S WYND *1903*

The shop advertising provisions on the right at 53 Perth Road belongs to James Aitken & Son. The family business was established in 1874 and has been trading at the same address ever since. Millers Wynd leads up to the right in front of the shop. The left tramcar was heading for West Park or Ninewells. The right tramcar was making for the High Street.

Park Terrace from Top of Seymour Street, Dundee.

Perth Road, Dundee

ABOVE: *NETHERGATE 1921*

This shows the Nethergate in the evening bustling with people in contrast to earlier pictures. Outside the City Churches a line of motor taxis awaits customers. To the right is the spire of St Paul's Church. To the left two shops can just be seen, 62 Nethergate belonged to J. M. Connel and Sons (bootmakers), and 56 Nethergate belonged to Charles Kerr (pharmacist).

TOP RIGHT: *UNION HALL circa 1873*

The Union Hall, originally an English Episcopal Chapel, was designed by the local architect Samuel Bell in 1783. The site was sold. When the congregation left, the name was changed to "Union Hall" and the place was let for public meetings. It was demolished in August 1876 as a consequence of the 1871 Improvement Act.

BOTTOM RIGHT: *HIGH STREET circa 1907*

The fine building on the right was the Town House or "Pillars". The picture shows two tramcars. For many years each tram route was considered to end in the High Street even if a through town route operated. Until 1924 east-west tramcars stopped for 5 to 10 minutes in the city centre. The tramcars could pick up passengers anywhere en route, but could only let them off at stops inscribed "Tramway Station".

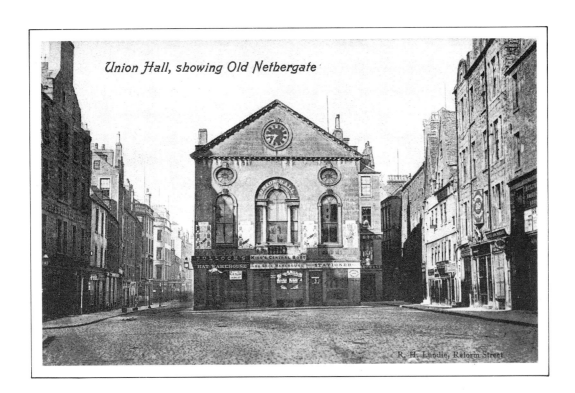

Union Hall, showing Old Nethergate

R. H. Lundie, Reform Street

High Street, Dundee.

ABOVE: *HIGH STREET circa 1907*

The Town House on the right was designed by William Adam (1688-1748), the father of the famous Adam brothers, in 1731. Completed in 1734, it contained the Council Chambers, associated offices, including the tramway offices, and an insecure town gaol. It was demolished in 1932. On 12 July 1900 the first electric tram ran from the High Street to West Park Road.

TOP RIGHT: *HIGH STREET circa 1905*

High Street was formerly known as Marketgait, meaning road to the market. Murraygait may have gained its name from Randolf, Earl of Moray. This thoroughfare was the main entrance to the town from the North. The Caird Fountain on the left of the picture was erected in 1879 by Edward Caird (1806-1889), father of Sir James Caird and founder in 1832 of the firm which developed into Ashton Jute Works, Hawkhill.

BOTTOM RIGHT: *HIGH STREET circa 1917*

The store on the right at 28 High Street belonged to Manfield & Sons, bootmakers. Philip Manfield, founder of this chain store, was the son of a Bristol shoemaker who became a skilled craftsman. In 1844, at the age of 25, he moved to Northampton with £100 of savings which he invested in a factory. By 1920 Manfield & Sons had 44 branches in the U.K. At 21 High Street can be seen Laird & Sinclair Ltd., nurserymen.

High Street, Dundee

No. 46   High Street Dundee   "Adelphi Series"

ABOVE: REFORM STREET circa 1903
Strathtay House, on the corner of Reform Street and the Old Overgate, were the premises of Adam Smail
"Home and Colonial" Outfitters from the early 1870s. The opposite corner, at 1 Reform Street, was occupied
by H. and W. Tulloch, hatters, founded around 1820. The business continued until 1909 when the site
was bought by H. Samuel, the jewellers.

TOP RIGHT: REFORM STREET circa 1914
Reform Street was designed by architect George Angus of Edinburgh in 1832 after an earlier proposal
in 1824-25 by architect William Burn. The street was opened in 1833 and named after the 1832 Reform
Bill. George Angus also designed the High School and Court House buildings in Bell Street. This card
was published by J. B. White of the Cowgate.

BOTTOM RIGHT: TRADES HALL circa 1878
The Trades Hall, opened in September 1778, was designed by Samuel Bell, the first city architect on
record. It was used as a meeting place for the Nine Trades of Dundee. The building was demolished on 4
April 1878 under the Improvement Act. The work was carried out through the night, with the aid of an
electric light, so as not too impede traffic.

Reform Street, Dundee.

Old Trades Hall, High Street, Dundee

Murraygate, Dundee

ABOVE: MURRAYGATE circa 1903
The Clydesdale Bank on the right was designed by William Spence in 1876. The canopies on the left belong to D. M. Brown's department store. The tramcar was making its way to the High Street. The route from High Street to Maryfield was opened on 6 March 1900. There was double track to Stobswell and single track with loops thereafter.

TOP RIGHT: MURRAYGATE circa 1907
On the right at 21 Murraygate were J. Hepworth & Sons Ltd. On the left was G. L. Wilson, "The Corner". In 1894, Gavine Laurie Wilson, a draper from Fife, opened a store at the corner of Murraygate and Commercial Street, which expanded into the space for eight shops. His son, Sir Garnet Wilson (1885-1975) was Lord Provost between 1940 and 1946, and contributed to education and the development of the city.

BOTTOM RIGHT: MURRAYGATE circa 1915
The founder of "The Globe" was Dundee-born Daniel S. Smith who later was appointed Bailie. He started up in 1884, taking his two brothers into partnership. Their first shop was at 35 Reform Street. In 1891 they expanded into a former public house called "The Globe", then moved to larger premises at 3-15 Murraygate in 1897 and retained the name of "The Globe".

V. 250-2   DUNDEE. MURRAYGATE.   RAPID PHOTO, E.C.

Murraygate, Dundee.

Murraygate, Dundee.

MURRAYGATE, DUNDEE

ABOVE: MURRAYGATE circa 1914
On the left at 30 Murraygate was La Scala Picture Theatre. Designed by George Boswell of Glasgow, it was opened on 9 December 1913 by Lord Provost Urquhart. Continuous performances ran daily from 2.30 p.m. until 10.30 p.m. Prices were 3d., 6d. or 1s. La Scala pioneered talkies when they were introduced in 1930. The cinema closed on 1 May 1965. The first cinema in Dundee was the Stobswell Cinema on Morgan Street, which was opened by Peter Feathers in 1910.

TOP RIGHT: MURRAYGATE LOOKING TOWARDS HIGH STREET circa 1917
On the right at 78 Murraygate "Corner of Murraygate" was G. H. Rowbottom, the tailor. Mr Rowbottom was born in Cambridge, became a manager of an Edinburgh clothing store and around 1898 came north to Dundee. He opened a shop in the Murraygate, which operated successfully until after the First World War. This card was published by Charles Helmrich & Sons of 22 Adelphi, Aberdeen.

BOTTOM RIGHT: WELLGATE circa 1906
The Wellgate took its name from the Lady Well, one of the three main water sources into Dundee until the mid-19th century. The picture shows a view looking up towards the Wellgate Steps. All the buildings in the picture have been replaced by the Wellgate Centre, designed in 1977.

No. 47   Murraygate, Dundee, looking to High Street "Adelphi S..."

113   WELLGATE, DUNDEE.   IDEAL SERIES.

Wishart Arch, Dundee

1491

R. H. Lundie, Reform Street

ABOVE: WISHART ARCH, COWGATE *circa 1873*

The cobblestones, gas lamps and Wishart Arch still preserve the atmosphere of the Old Cowgate. Wishart Arch is on the site of the 16th century Cowgate Port and the present Arch may contain elements of the old port. The reformer, George Wishart (c. 1513-1545), had preached in this area to the plague victims of 1544.

TOP RIGHT: VICTORIA ROAD AT THE FOOT OF HILLTOWN *1903*

On the right above the Wellgate Steps John Robertson advertised himself as a tooth manufacturer. On the left at 22 Victoria Road, Alex Inglis, wine and spirit merchant, advertised free snacks sold with Allsop's Ale. Tramcar No. 21 was heading into the city centre despite displaying the sign "Fairmuir". In 1903 the fare from Commercial Street to Fairmuir would have been 1 ½d. inside, 1d. outside.

BOTTOM RIGHT: VICTORIA ROAD *1914*

This was a busy road which linked the many jute mills in the area with the docks. Jute carts shown on the left of the picture carried rolls of sacking and bales of raw jute to the mills. Jute carts on the right were returning to town and then to the docks with the manufactured products. Victoria Road in comparison to the Wellgate was lit by regularly spaced gas street lamps on both sides.

40732 Victoria Road, Dundee.   Valentines Series

Victoria Road, Dundee.   79326 J.V.

ABOVE: HEAD OF HILLTOWN 1903

The well-known landmark, the tap-o' the hill clock, shown in the centre of the picture, was presented by Bailie Charles Barrie to the community in 1900. The clock was supplied by G. D. Rattray of the Nethergate. The gas-lit dial was turned on for the first time on 21 September 1901. In front of the clock, No. 53 single deck "Conshie", Constitution Road, tramcar was heading into town.

TOP RIGHT: FOOT OF HILLTOWN 1904

A view down towards the Wellgate Steps and Victoria Road. The River Tay can be seen in the distance. Trams never ran on this part of Hilltown because of the steepness of the road. They joined Hilltown at a higher level from Constitution Street en route to Fairmuir. Extra horses were kept at the foot of Hilltown to assist heavy cartloads up the hill.

BOTTOM RIGHT: BUCKLEMAKER WYND — NOW VICTORIA ROAD circa 1870

The photograph was taken at the junction of the Wellgate and the Hilltown, with Bucklemaker Wynd leading off into the distance. The Bucklemakers were a branch of the Hammermen, one of the Nine Trades of Dundee. They made buckles for a variety of purposes including saddlery, sword-belts and shoes. Members of the same craft tended to live in the same area.

Foot of Hilltown, Dundee.

R. H. Lundie, Reform Street

*Bucklemaker Wynd (now Victoria Road),
Dundee*

TOP OF HILLTOWN *circa 1906*
FOOT OF HILLTOWN *circa 1907*

HILLTOWN, DUNDEE.

IDEAL SERIES.

Foot of Hilltown, Dundee

TOP OF HILLTOWN *circa 1905*
FOOT OF HILLTOWN *circa 1920*

R. H. Lundie, Reform Street

In the Vault, Dundee

Union Street (now site of Mathers' Hotel), Dundee

ABOVE: CHOLERA HOSPITAL circa 1873

The Cholera Hospital on the left stood where the Tay Hotel is today. It was built as a tenement, but the Corporation took it over as an isolation hospital when the Infirmary in King Street could not cope with the cholera victims during the epidemic in 1832. Many people died and were buried in common graves in the Howff. After the outbreak the building reverted to tenements. It was demolished when the Whitehall Crescent area was developed in the 1880s.

LEFT: THE VAULT circa 1873

Behind the old Town House was a narrow passageway called the Vault. It connected the High Street with the Greenmarket. The Vault was so named because it was the kirkyard of St Clement's Church, which was superseded when the Howff opened as a cemetery in 1564.

Castle Court, Dundee

Old Custom House and Fish Streeet, Dundee

R. H. Lundie, Reform Street

ABOVE: OLD CUSTOM HOUSE AND FISH STREET circa 1873

The Old Custom House, built in the 16th century, had once been the town house of Provost Pierson. Originally it had three towers, similar in design to those of Dudhope Castle, but these had to be removed in the 17th century. In 1808 a mason carrying out maintenance on the building discovered a hoard of silver coins. These may have been hidden during the siege of Dundee in 1651. In the late 18th century the building was used as a Custom House. The new Custom House was built in 1843 in Dock Street.

LEFT: CASTLE COURT circa 1873

The picture shows Castle Court with the spire of St Paul's Cathedral in the background. A prominent feature of the tenements shown are the washing poles projecting from the windows. It took until 1876 before the city had an adequate water supply. Thereafter sanitation in millworkers' houses improved. It was not until around 1888 that it became common for tenements to have W.C.s.

Head of Seagate, Dundee

R. H. Lundie, Reform Street

91

ABOVE: SEAGATE circa 1871

The Seagate was the heart of Old Dundee in medieval times. The city expanded westward, and in the late 18th century the docks expanded eastward and the Seagate became more industrialised. The Mercat Cross was originally erected, in the mid-13th century, in the Seagate. At 99 Seagate a plaque marks the site of the birthplace of Sarah Wiedeman, the mother of poet Robert Browning.

TOP RIGHT: OVERGATE, 12 May 1898

A view along the old Overgate towards St Paul's Cathedral. The shop at No. 25, behind the horse and cart, belonged to Lindsay and Low, confectioners. Sir James Low (1849-1923) became Lord Provost of Dundee between 1893 and 1896. The firm evolved into William Low & Co. when Sir James' brother, William, developed the firm which flourishes today.

BOTTOM RIGHT: OVERGATE circa 1903

The picture shows John Ramsay's confectionery shop and tearooms at 11 Overgate. The old Overgate, which was full of character, does not survive today. The construction of the new Overgate was the first town centre redevelopment in Scotland. It was built in three stages and completed in April 1970 when it was formally opened by H.R.H. Princess Margaret. The whole development cost £4 million.

44

Whitehall Street, Dundee   Valentines Series

ABOVE: *WHITEHALL STREET circa 1903*

Whitehall Street was opened as a fashionable shopping area in the late 1880s, replacing several old closes. One of the houses belonged to Sir Patrick Lyon of Carse, a second cousin of the first Earl of Strathmore. As an ardent Royalist, he changed the name of his house to "Whitehall" at the restoration of Charles II in 1660. Thus Whitehall gained its name.

TOP RIGHT: *WHITEHALL CRESCENT circa 1907*

Whitehall Crescent was built during the period 1885-1889. On the right below Mather's Temperance Hotel at 34 Whitehall Crescent were Peebles Bros., grocers, founded in 1886 by John and David Peebles. John played a prominent part in the introduction of the weekly half-holiday for shop assistants throughout the country.

BOTTOM RIGHT: *SOUTH UNION STREET circa 1910*

The drinking fountain shown here was presented by William Longair, Lord Provost between 1905 and 1908, to commemorate two Royal visits to Dundee during his term of office. To the right of the young lad with the bicycle are three street urchins wandering around the town barefoot. The clock tower belonged to the Caledonian Railway Station.

Whitehall Crescent, Dundee.

Alexandra Fountain and S. Union Street, Dundee

ABOVE: UNION STREET circa 1905

On the right was Mather's Temperance Hotel where D. B. Mathers was managing director. It was designed in 1898 by Robert Hunter. The Mather family kept a temperance coffee house on the Murraygate. In the 1880s, when the new street through Whitehall was being laid out, the Burgh Council approached the Mathers and offered them a loan to set up business running a new hotel there.

TOP RIGHT: FAIRMUIR TERMINUS 1913

A view along Clepington Road from Strathmartine Road. In 1911 the Town Council decided to install trackless trolley cars which ran along Clepington Road from Maryfield to Strathmartine Road. The service commenced on 5 September 1911 and the fare charged between termini was 1d. The dust stirred up by these vehicles earned the trolley cars the nickname of "Stouries". They were discontinued in May 1914.

BOTTOM RIGHT: WATSON STREET AND FERRY ROAD circa 1905

Tramcar No. 9, shown here, was heading out to Monifieth. The route ran from Dundee High Street to Craigie Terrace via Seagate, Blackcroft, Broughty Ferry Road and Springhill. On 11 November 1901 the route to Springhill was opened. Most of the track stayed in place after the route closed in May 1931, until it was required during the Second World War.

New Railless Trolley Car from Fairmuir Terminus, Dundee.

Star Series.

Watson Street and Ferry Road, Dundee.

Star Series.

49

WINDSOR STREET 1896
PEDDIE STREET circa 1907

STOBSWELL *circa 1910*
STOBSWELL LOOKING DOWN ALBERT STREET *circa 1925*

ABOVE: *BAXTER PARK TERRACE circa 1904*
The picture shows a view of Baxter Park Terrace with the Morgan Academy in the distance. To the right lies Baxter Park. A horse-drawn tram service to Baxter Park from Victoria Bridge began on 18 June 1880. This card is one of the "Reliable" series published by Edinburgh's most prolific postcard publisher, William Ritchie & Sons Ltd.

TOP RIGHT: *HIGH STREET, LOCHEE 1901*
The crowded scene shows a change of shift at Cox's Camperdown Works, seen in the distance with the famous Cox's Stack, built in 1865. Lochee High Street was the terminus for Dundee trams. A horse-tram service started running from Tay Street to Lochee on 23 December 1879. Normal electric tram services ceased in Dundee on 20 October 1956 with the closure of the Perth Road, Maryfield and Lochee routes.

BOTTOM RIGHT: *DOCK STREET LOOKING WEST circa 1910*
Dock Street was an important thoroughfare which gave access to the harbour from the city centre. The famous civil engineer Thomas Telford was appointed to design the first harbour improvements. His new West Graving Dock opened on 24 December 1823. King William IV Dock, shown here on the left, opened two years later, and Earl Grey Dock was completed in November 1834.

High Street (North End), Lochee

Dock Street, looking W., Dundee

Dock Street,   Dundee.

ABOVE: DOCK STREET circa 1905

On the right of the picture in the distance can be seen the Custom House and the old East Station. On the left can be seen the building which belonged to George Morton Ltd, distillers, brewers, wine and whisky merchants. Whisky was never distilled in Dundee but a number of firms stored and blended spirits. The original George Morton founded the firm in 1838, which developed from a grocery business.

TOP RIGHT: THE DOCKS circa 1878

The picture shows the Tide Harbour in the foreground. The three-storey square building in the centre was the Dockmaster's Office. Earl Grey Dock was situated to the left, King William IV Dock to the right. By the 1880s the docks were unsuitable for large fully-laden jute ships so the Western and Eastern Wharves were built. Further extensions to the docks in the 20th century were George V and Princess Alexandra Wharves.

BOTTOM RIGHT: ROYAL ARCH 1878

The success of the harbour improvements was celebrated by a Royal visit. A temporary Royal Arch, designed by harbour engineer James Leslie, was hurriedly made of wood. Queen Victoria, Prince Albert and the Princess Royal landed in Dundee on 11 September 1844 and toured some of the principal streets. In 1850 the Arch was reconstructed in sandstone. It was demolished in 1964 to make way for the Tay Bridge approach roads.

Valentines Series

The Docks, Dundee

Royal Arch, Dundee

Valentines Series

ABOVE: *BALAENA circa 1895*

The "whaler" *Balaena* was built in Norway and joined the Dundee fleet in 1891, where she operated as a whaler until 1917. Dundee's interest in Arctic whaling began around 1750 with the formation of the Tay Whale and Fishing Company. By the second half of the 19th century Dundee had the finest fleet in the country. Scarcity of whales and replacement of whale oil in the jute industry by the 1890s caused the industry to decline.

TOP RIGHT: *H.M.S. UNICORN, EARL GREY DOCK circa 1905*

H.M.S. *Unicorn* was launched at the Royal Dockyard, Chatham, on 30 March 1824 and is the oldest British-built ship afloat. In November 1873 she was towed to Dundee where she served as the R.N.R. and R.N.V.R. Drill Ship. During both world wars she was the base for the Senior Naval Officer in Dundee. In 1968 she was handed over to the Unicorn Preservation Trust for restoration.

BOTTOM RIGHT: *R.S.S. DISCOVERY LEAVING DOCK AFTER HER OFFICIAL LAUNCH 1901*

The *Discovery* was built by Dundee Shipbuilders Co. Ltd for the National Antarctic Expedition Committee at a cost of £51,000. Captain Robert Falcon Scott (1868-1912) was appointed Commander in 1900. On 21 March 1901 *Discovery* was launched and underwent sea trials on the Tay.

DUNDEE.   H. M. S. UNICORN.

DISCOVERY - LEAVING THE DOCK.   35348 JV.

ABOVE: R.S.S. DISCOVERY DURING SEA TRIALS ON THE TAY 1901
The *Discovery* left London docks at the end of July 1901 bound for New Zealand, before moving on to McMurdo Sound. In January 1904, after being iced in for two winters, she was rescued by the *Terra Nova* and the *Morning*, both from Dundee. Scott returned to the Antarctic on his ill-fated 1910-12 expedition on the smaller *Terra Nova*. The *Discovery* returned to Dundee in 1986 for restoration and display.

TOP RIGHT: THE DOCKS *circa 1910*
Dock Street originally marked the line of the River Tay before reclamation began. By 1836 the volume of shipping precipitated the dock's expansion. Camperdown Dock opened on 20 July 1865 and Victoria Dock opened on 16 August 1875. They were both deeper docks, better equipped with warehousing, and both survive today.

BOTTOM RIGHT: HARBOUR *circa 1905*
The town and harbour were linked with a railway system. Lines were laid along the quays of King William IV and Earl Grey Docks and the system was extended as the harbour grew. Every part of the harbour became linked up and some firms had their own private sidings. By 1930 there were about 14 miles of railway lines which belonged to the Harbour trustees.

Dundee from the Docks

Dundee Harbour, from the River

Craig Pier, Dundee

ABOVE: *CRAIG PIER circa 1903*
The picture shows the Tay ferry *Fifeshire* which was built in Glasgow in 1858 for £7,000. She remained in service until she was scrapped in 1929. The last 'Fifie' to be constructed was the *Scotscraig*. She was built in 1951 by the Caledon Yard, Dundee. On the 18th August 1966 she made the last crossing of the Tay, decorated in flags, having been superseded by the opening of the Tay Road Bridge.

TOP RIGHT: *P.S. 'MARCHIONESS OF BUTE' circa 1910*
The picture shows P.S. *Marchioness of Bute*. She was built in 1890 for the Caledonian Steam Packet Co. Ltd (1888-1922) and operated principally from Wemyss Bay. In July 1908 she was sold to D. and J. Nicol for excursions on the Tay. She was stationed at Portsmouth as a minesweeper during the war. After this she was kept at Inverkeithing and broken up in 1923.

BOTTOM RIGHT: *TAY BRIDGE AND ESPLANADE STATION circa 1904*
Postcards of the Tay Bridge and Docks were withdrawn from circulation by autumn 1916, until after the First World War. Censorship of postcards also occurred during the Second World War. This prevented unnecessary use of raw materials and allowed industrial sites to be used to help the war effort. At this time Valentine's Westfield Works was converted to the manufacture of machine tools.

No. 50　　Entrance to Tidal Basin, Dundee Docks　"Adelphi Series"

Tay Bridge, and Esplanade Station, Dundee.　　RELIABLE SERIES. 02095

PATENT SLIP, DUNDEE.

ABOVE: PATENT SLIP *circa 1905*
The Tay ferry *Dundee* is here being overhauled at Dundee's Patent Slip. Built at Renfrew in 1875 at a cost of £8,700, she served on the Tay crossing until 1917. She was then bought by the Tay Steam Boat Co. and for the next three years she ran pleasure cruises up stream. The remainder of her career was spent on the River Forth. In 1952 she was finally sold to ship breakers at Charlestown, near Rosyth.

TOP RIGHT: S.S. PANAMA *1912*
In 1912 the Dundee Shipbuilding Co. Ltd. launched seven vessels and 12 barges. The largest vessel built that year was the S.S. *Panama*. On completion this steamship was engaged in passenger, cargo and cattle transport between Central and Southern America.

BOTTOM RIGHT: THE LAW *1905*
The Law is the plug or core of an extinct volcano, and rises from sea level to a height of 571 feet. It was acquired from private ownership by the Town Council in 1879 and made into a recreational area for the city. The War Memorial, commemorating the First World War, was unveiled by General Sir Ian Hamilton on 16 May 1925.

S.S. "PANAMA."
Built by the Dundee Shipbuilding Co., Ltd., Dundee, 1912.

Law Hill   Dundee

THE INNER BASIN circa 1908
THE DOCKS circa 1905

FISHWIVES IN DUNDEE MARKET.

FISHWIVES IN THE GREENMARKET circa 1908
The Greenmarket, now absorbed into the site of the Caird Hall, had originally been the Fish Market. The fish were caught locally at the mouth of the River Tay and around the coast of Fife. Fish included haddock, cod, flounders, skate, and sometimes turbot. The fishwives came on Tuesdays, Fridays and Saturdays to sell fish from their baskets. Women from Arbroath brought in crabs, lobsters, shellfish and dried fish. These women walked into Dundee and back again at the end of their day. With no refrigeration the quality of fish sometimes left much to be desired.

ABOVE: MURRAYGATE circa 1905

The picture shows a tramcar making its way to the High Street. The first Sunday tram service ran on 10 September 1905 but, in order to prevent disturbances during church services, did not run between 11 a.m. and 12.10 p.m.

TOP RIGHT: HARBOUR AND ROYAL ARCH circa 1906

The picture was painted by artist David Small (1846-1927). He worked as a photographer and illustrator in Dundee. This is one of a set of six "Oilette" postcards published by Raphael Tuck and Sons Ltd, of London. The artist also supplied paintings of Edinburgh, Fife, Glasgow, and the Clyde Coast , which they published as postcards.

BOTTOM RIGHT: HIGH STREET 1934

The Caird hall, off to the left, was opened by H.R.H. Prince Edward, Prince of Wales, on 26 October 1923. H.R.H. Prince George opened the new City Chambers, which occupy the west wing of the Square, on 30 November 1933. Artist G. W. Blow painted this picture which was used by Valentine.

Dundee Harbour and Royal Arch. D. Small.

HIGH STREET, DUNDEE.

Dudhope Castle, Dundee

ABOVE: *DUDHOPE CASTLE circa 1903*

In 1792 the castle was sub-let to a woollen company which went bankrupt. In 1795 the Government leased the castle and grounds for 95 years. It was used as an army barracks until August 1880. In 1892 the estate was bought by the Town Council and private individuals for £317,000.

TOP RIGHT: *ROYAL INFIRMARY circa 1904*

The Royal Infirmary opened on 22 February 1855. Funds for its construction were raised mainly by public subscription. It relied on public financial support until 1948 when it came under the control of the East of Scotland Health Board. Ninewells Hospital, with 800 beds, became the main hospital in the city when it was opened by the Queen Mother in 1974.

BOTTOM RIGHT: *WISHART ARCH circa 1904*

Through the archway, which was extensively restored in 1877, was the Wishart Chapel which Mary Slessor (1848-1915) attended. Mary Slessor, born in Aberdeen, moved to Dundee in 1859 at the age of 11 years. She worked in Baxter's Mill as a "half-timer" before becoming a missionary in Calabar, Nigeria, in 1876.

The Infirmary, Dundee.

Wishart Arch, Dundee.

TAY BRIDGE. DUNDEE.

ABOVE: TAY BRIDGE AND ESPLANADE STATION 1934

The Esplanade Station, at Buckingham Point, opened in 1889. In 1887 the public authorities obtained parliamentary powers to reclaim land from the River Tay from Buckingham Point, Magdalen Green, as far west as Ninewells. Before reclamation the Caledonian Railway ran along the edge of the shore.

TOP RIGHT: BAXTER PARK 1905

David Baxter was knighted in the New Year's Honours List of 1863 in recognition of his position in the linen industry and his benefaction of Baxter Park. A statue presented to Sir David now stands in the entrance of the McManus Galleries in Albert Square, Dundee. Baxter Park was handed over to the Town Council in 1878 for maintenance.

BOTTOM RIGHT: HIGH STREET circa 1903

The picture shows three electric open-topped trams in the foreground. Top covers had been standard in the early steam trams of the 1880s. Many people disliked the open-topped electric trams when they were brought into service. Top-roofs were gradually introduced to the tram fleet between 1905 and 1910.

Entrance to Baxter Park from Arbroath Road   Dundee

High Street, Dundee

The Law from
Balgay Hill, Dundee

The Esplanade   Dundee

The Sunlit Docks, Dundee. 90

ABOVE: *THE SUNLIT DOCKS circa 1908*

The picture shows small fishing boats which were used to catch sprats. A quick sale of the catch was necessary since the fish rapidly deteriorated. Old fish were sold to make fertiliser at a lower price. The Dundee registration on the boats can be clearly seen.

TOP LEFT: *THE LAW 1903*

The Law was the site of a vitrified hillfort probably occupied during the Bronze Age. Remains of the settlement were found where the road was built to the top of the Law in the 1920s. Over the centuries it had been occupied by the Picts and the Scots.

BOTTOM LEFT: *ESPLANADE circa 1905*

A plaque was unveiled on the Esplanade, near the old Esplanade Station, by Lord Provost Tom Mitchell, J.P., on 20th June 1987 to commemorate the 100th anniversary of the first passenger train to cross the second Tay Bridge. The plaque is mounted on the coping stone from Pier 12 of the original bridge.

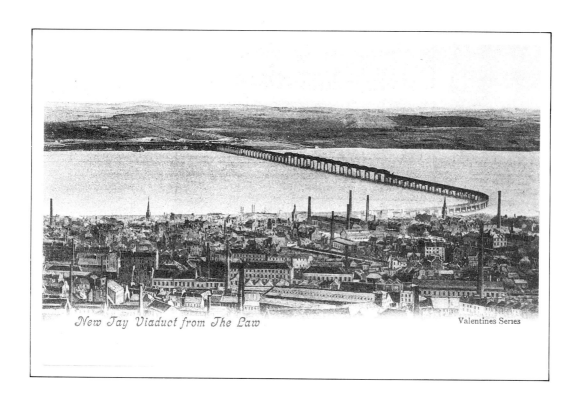

New Tay Viaduct from The Law   Valentines Series

ABOVE: TAY BRIDGE FROM THE LAW circa 1903

The dominant features here are the vast jute mills and associated mill chimneys of which at least 20 can be counted. In 1865 an observer standing on the Law counted about 120 factory chimneys. A commanding panoramic view can be obtained from the summit of the Law, of Forfarshire, Fife, Perthshire, Inverness-shire and even the Grampian range of Aberdeenshire.

TOP RIGHT: ESPLANADE circa 1903

The Esplanade was constructed and opened, as far as the Tay Railway Bridge, in 1875. It was subsequently extended in stages westward. The Second Tay Railway Bridge visible in the distance was built at a cost of £640,000. The first Railway Bridge cost £270,000 and was destroyed in a storm on 28 December 1879.

BOTTOM RIGHT: ESPLANADE LOOKING EAST circa 1903

On the left can be seen the clock tower of the fine Caledonian Railway Station. In the distance stood Mather's Temperance Hotel which is now the Tay Hotel. In 1901 the Prohibitionist Party was founded in Dundee with Edwin Scrymgeour as leader. Scrymgeour became the first and only Prohibitionist M.P., sensationally defeating Winston Churchill in 1922.

VALENTINES SERIES

Esplanade, Dundee

Thursday.   4.6.03.

Dundee.   The Esplanade (East End)

Valentines Series   1048

DUDHOPE CASTLE, DUNDEE

ABOVE: DUDHOPE CASTLE circa 1912

Dudhope Castle was the principal seat of the Scrymgeours, hereditary Constables of Dundee. In 1298 King John granted the land of Dudhope to Sir Alexander Scrymgeour as a reward for resisting the English. Around 1460 the old keep was replaced with a fortified castle. In the 16th century Sir James Scrymgeour, the then Constable of Dundee, built the present L-shaped castle to replace the earlier castle.

TOP RIGHT: BARRACK PARK circa 1903

The picture shows the entrance to Barrack Park from Lochee Road. Looking through the park from the left to right could be seen the Deaf and Dumb School, now demolished, the Royal Infirmary and Dudhope Castle. The officers' quarters, beyond the castle, served as an industrial museum from 1900-1939. After lying vacant for several years the castle has recently been restored.

BOTTOM RIGHT: THE TIME GUN circa 1911

Dundee's time gun was situated at Dudhope Castle in Dudhope Park. It was fired daily at one o'clock from the 1870s until February 1916. The firing was stopped because it was causing distress to soldiers who were recuperating in the nearby Royal Infirmary. After 1924 it was used again but only on Hogmanay and Armistice Day until it was finally silenced in 1936.

Entrance to Barrack Park, Dundee

Valentines Series

The Time Gun
Dundee

Dudhope Barracks and Gymnasium.   *Dundee.*

ABOVE: DUDHOPE BARRACKS AND GYMNASIUM *circa 1904*

Dudhope Park, also known as Barrack Park, was opened to the public on 28 September 1895 by Lord Provost Sir James Low. A special feature was the open-air gymnasium for children under 14 years old. This had been erected in Barrack Square at a cost of £200.

TOP RIGHT: NORTH GATE, BALGAY PARK *circa 1875*

Balgay Park was acquired around 1869 by the Town Council from Sir William and Lady Scott of Ancrum. The west part of Balgay Park was laid out as a cemetery and the east part as a park. A cast-iron bridge of three arches was constructed across the valley dividing the two parts. This can be seen in the picture. The park was opened in September 1871 by the Earl of Dalhousie.

BOTTOM RIGHT: PAVILION, BALGAY PARK *circa 1904*

In 1871 the west portion of Balgay Park, behind the pavilion, was laid out as a cemetery. Earlier that century, the Howff in Meadowside was used as a burial ground and around 1837 Constitution Road Cemetery opened. In 1847 the Western Cemetery opened and in 1864 the Eastern Necropolis was opened.

Balgay Park, Dundee.

104. J.V.

Funeral of the late Col. Smith, V.D. 25/8/05   Valentines Series

ABOVE: FUNERAL OF THE LATE COL. SMITH, V.D., 16th August 1905
Colonel William Smith, V.D., born 10th March 1844, died at Binn Cottage, Perth Road, on 13th August 1905. About a fortnight before he had been at Barry Camp where he had developed appendicitis which became peritonitis. The family requested a military funeral which was the biggest ever in Dundee. The memorial service was held in St Mary's Parish Church. Afterwards the coffin was carried to a gun-carriage and the cortege started its journey to the Western Cemetery. The Nethergate and Perth Road, from St Mary's Church right out to the Western Cemetery, were lined with thousands of people.

TOP RIGHT: BARRACK PARK circa 1905
Barrack Square was enclosed by iron railings and divided into two sections, one for boys, nearest the castle, and one for girls. In the boys' section, the apparatus included a giant stride, two parallel bars, a vaulting horse, a horizontal bar plus ladder, four pairs of rings, six swings and a number of see-saws. The girls' side differed slightly in the choice of apparatus.

BOTTOM RIGHT: PAVILION, BALGAY PARK circa 1903
In 1871 the west portion of Balgay Park was laid out as a cemetery. A hearse was rarely used, except by the better off, until around 1857. Coffins were covered with a pall, called a mortcloth, and carried on two black spikes. The attendants walked behind. The "saulie", dressed in a long black gown and cocked hat, marched in front clearing the way.

Dundee from Balgay Hill

Valentines Series 51404

ABOVE: VIEW FROM BALGAY HILL 1905
The spire of St Paul's Cathedral and the tower of the Old Steeple are seen above the numerous mill chimneys here. Early 19th century houses had one or two storeys, superseded by three- or four-storey tenements. Tenements were provided with backcourts which contained washhouses, coalsheds, middens and sometimes outside W.C.s.

TOP RIGHT: MILLS OBSERVATORY 1935
The Mills Observatory, built in 1935, is situated on the summit of Balgay Hill. John Mills (1806-1889) was a manufacturer of linen and twine in the city and a keen amateur astronomer. In his will he left instruction for a public observatory to be built, and Balgay Hill was selected as the most suitable site.

BOTTOM RIGHT: BAXTER PARK 1905
David Baxter (1793-1872) started his career in sugar refining. He became one of the partners of the family linen firm Baxter Bros. & Co. Ltd, and funded a park in memory of his father. The park was laid out and designed by Sir Joseph Paxton, who designed Chatsworth House and Crystal Palace, at a cost of £50,000, and was formally opened on 9 September 1863.

MILLS OBSERVATORY, DUNDEE.

Baxter Park, Dundee

Baxter Park, Dundee.

ABOVE: BAXTER PARK *circa 1914*

In 1822 Baxters erected a spinning mill at Lower Dens in Dundee which made use of the water power from the culverted Dens Burn. Assisted by engineer and inventor Peter Carmichael, Baxters introduced powerweaving in 1836 which was used for linen manufacture before it was adopted for jute. Their business was almost exclusively textiles of flax and hemp.

TOP RIGHT: PAVILION, BAXTER PARK *circa 1903*

Baxters reached the peak of their prosperity in 1871 when they employed some 5,000 workers, which was 2,000 more workers than Cox Bros, of Lochee. Baxters became a limited company in 1892. The firm became a member of the Low & Bonar Group in 1924 and they ceased trading in 1974.

BOTTOM RIGHT: LOCHEE PARK *1898*

Lochee Park lies to the north of Balgay Hill. It was presented by Cox Bros., who owned Camperdown Jute Works, in 1899 and was partly endowed by them. Cox Bros. bought the 25-acre site for £10,000. In addition they spent £3,500 on building the lodge, surrounding boundary walls, railings, and preparing the ground for football, cricket and other sports.

Pavilion Baxter Park, Dundee

Entrance, Lochee Park

28574

ABOVE: MAGDALEN GREEN 1905

In earlier times the green led down to a beach which was popular for bathing and boating. In 1845 the Dundee and Perth Railway Line cut off the "Green" from the river. The innovation of the railway was welcomed by most people but caused annoyance to park users and swimmers. The fine Victorian bandstand made from cast iron was constructed in 1889.

TOP RIGHT: THE TRIANGLE, MAGDALEN GREEN 1913

It was in the area of Paton's Lane and Step Row that William McGonagall lived. McGonagall was born in Edinburgh of Irish parentage around 1825. His father moved to Dundee in search of work when William was still young. William was later employed as a handloom weaver. In June 1877 he started to write verse of contemporary events such as the Tay Bridge and Tay Whale.

BOTTOM RIGHT: STOBSMUIR POND circa 1909

Stobsmuir Pond is situated at the northeast end of the city near Maryfield. The name Stobsmuir is derived from "stob", meaning a stump of a tree or a stake, and "muir", which is a Scottish name for waste or barren land. There were two ponds at Stobsmuir that were used for sailing model yachts. In the winter the ponds were used for skating.

The Triangle, Magdalen Green, Dundee

JV 75364

Stobsmuir Pond, Dundee.

JV 57283.

Mains Castle, near Dundee   Valentines Series

ABOVE: MAINS CASTLE circa 1903
Sir David Graham of Fintry finished the building of Mains Castle in 1582, construction having been started by his father. In 1788 David Erskine acquired the castle. In 1912 Sir James Key Caird (1837-1916) bought the ruinous Mains Castle and surrounding estate. Caird Park was formally opened on 27 October 1920 by Mrs Marryat, sister of Sir James Caird. Sir James Caird died on 10 March 1916.

TOP RIGHT: HIGH SCHOOL, EUCLID CRESCENT circa 1905
The history of the High School goes back to 1239 when the Abbot of Lindores was instructed to build a grammar school in the new burgh of Dundee. In 1589 the school received its first permanent home in St Clement's Lane, where it remained for exactly 200 years. The present school, shown in the picture, was designed by George Angus of Edinburgh and was opened on 1 October 1834.

BOTTOM RIGHT: MORGAN ACADEMY circa 1914
Morgan Academy was founded by John Morgan who was born in Dundee in 1760. By 1812 he had amassed a large fortune as an indigo planter in India which enabled him to retire and return to Dundee. He died in 1850 aged 90. He left money in his will for the building of the Morgan Hospital. The boarding school opened on 5 February 1868 with 90 boys.

High School   Dundee

MORGAN ACADEMY, DUNDEE   E.03097

ABOVE: HARRIS ACADEMY, PARK PLACE *circa 1912*

Baillie William Harris, a wealthy and respected corn-merchant and mill owner, offered the School Board £10,000 to build the Harris Academy in Park Place. The Academy opened to pupils on 31 August 1885 when 1,035 pupils were enrolled. By 1888 1,500 pupils attended. A new school was required. The new Harris Academy opened on its present site on Perth Road on 1 May 1931.

TOP RIGHT: HARRIS ACADEMY INFANTS' DRILL *circa 1898*

The original Park Place Harris had a wide pupil age range. Boys and girls were taught separately until they became very senior pupils. All classes were fee-paying at this time. Initially infant education cost five shillings a quarter. School uniform had not been introduced at this time. Infants were taught religious knowledge, reading, spelling, writing on slates, arithmetic, objective lessons, industrial work and singing.

BOTTOM RIGHT: UNIVERSITY COLLEGE *circa 1903*

It was through the generosity of Miss Mary Ann Baxter of Balgavies (1801-1884), who donated £120,000 from her share of the fortune from the family textile business, that University College was founded in 1881. A line of four detached town houses facing Nethergate, between Park Place and Small's Wynd, were acquired in 1881. The College was opened on 5 October 1883 by Lord Dalhousie.

University College, Dundee

University College, Dundee — Valentines Series

ABOVE: UNIVERSITY COLLEGE *circa 1903*

The building with the greenhouse formed the Department of Botany. The Chair of botany was founded in 1889 under Professor Patrick Geddes (1854-1932). In 1897 a union between the College and St Andrews University was established. In 1898 the Medical School was founded independently of the College. In 1954 University College was renamed Queens College and the Medical School became part of the College.

TOP RIGHT: CHEMISTRY LABORATORY *circa 1900*

The Chemistry Department was the only purpose-built building for the new College. It was paid for by a further gift of £10,000 from Miss Baxter. In 1882 Thomas Carnelley (1852-90) became the first Professor of Chemistry in Dundee where he set up the department and laboratories. The main laboratory shown in the picture was used by both elementary and advanced students.

BOTTOM RIGHT: WEST PORT *1903*

The road leading off to the right was the Scouringburn, later changed to Brook Street, which led into Polepark Road. Meadowside for many years until 1825 was the Public Bleaching Green with the water supply being the Scouring Burn which ran underground and joined Tod's Burn at the north of Commercial Street. The tram shown was heading into the city centre from Balgay Lodge.

1298   THE LABORATORY, UNIVERSITY COLLEGE, DUNDEE   VALENTINES SERIES

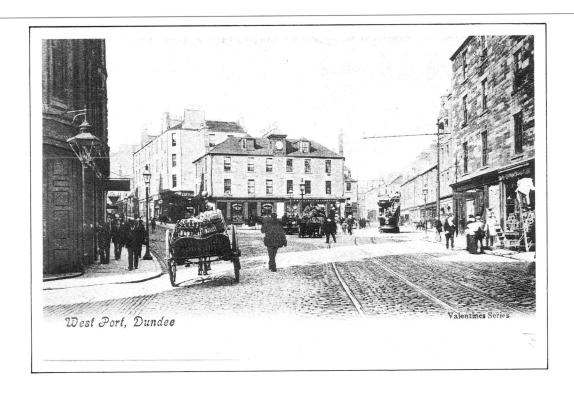

West Port, Dundee

Valentines Series

ST. PAUL'S CATHEDRAL CHURCH, DUNDEE

INTERIOR ST. PAUL'S CATHEDRAL, DUNDEE.

LEFT: ST PAUL'S CATHEDRAL, CASTLEHILL 1898

The castle of Dundee, destroyed c. 1314, formerly stood on the site of St Paul's Cathedral. It was here where William Wallace slew the son of the English Governor of Dundee Castle. The Cathedral was designed by Sir George Gilbert Scott in 1852. The two buildings which share Castlehill with the Cathedral are both part of the same complex. Castlehill House is a Georgian Townhouse and contains the Cathedral Office. St Roque's Hall, next door, was at one time the Episcopal School and now serves as a base for the Cathedral's social activities. Castlehill was the birthplace of Admiral Duncan (1731-1804) who defeated the Dutch fleet on the 14th October 1797 at a place called Kamperdoen on the Dutch coast. On his return he was made Viscount Camperdown and Baron of Lundie. With the money he received he built Camperdown House in 1824 and laid out the park. The estate passed through the family until they all died. It was bought by the Town Council with money from the Sir James Caird Acquisition Fund and opened to the public on 29th September 1946.

ABOVE: INTERIOR OF ST PAUL'S CATHEDRAL, circa 1903

The mosaic panel of the Annunciation behind the altar was in the Episcopal Church in Castle Street which was used before St Paul's was built. The chapel to the left of the chancel is dedicated to St Roque (St Roche), a French saint who cared for the sick in Italy during the Great Plague. The architect of the Cathedral, George Gilbert Scott (1811-1878), was the son of a Church of England clergyman. He designed his first church at Lincoln in 1838 and soon became established as a church architect. He was acknowledged as a great Gothic architect. He later went on to design St Mary's Episcopal Church, Broughty Ferry, in 1858 and the Albert Institute in 1865-7.7.

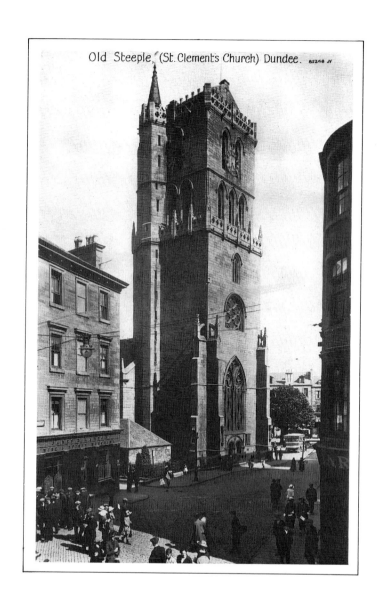

Old Steeple, (St. Clement's Church) Dundee.

Old Tower and Churches, Dundee

Valentines Series

LEFT: OLD STEEPLE, OR ST MARY'S TOWER 1921

The Old Steeple of St Mary's Church is the oldest surviving building in central Dundee. Lindsay Street in the foreground is now a pedestrian area. The buildings on the right and left were demolished to make way for the new Overgate precinct. St Mary's Church was founded at the end of the 12th century. It was later destroyed by fire when an English army under King Edward I captured and occupied the town. By the early 15th century progress on restoration was so slow that the Town Council assisted in the work, leading to completion of the Tower by the 1480s. In 1547-48 an English force, having taken possession of the castle at Broughty Ferry, captured Dundee, fortified St Mary's Tower and used the church for stables. Again the church was set on fire. The rafters and fire-cracked walls of the nave and transepts were demolished but the tower survived. In 1651 the Old Steeple was used by the defenders of Dundee in their last desperate stand against Cromwell's army under General Monk which later captured the town. The defenders were slain along with many citizens. The town's trade and wealth were destroyed or seized and it was not until the 1730s that Dundee began to recover from the disaster. Over a period of time the churches were rebuilt.

ABOVE: OLD STEEPLE AND CHURCHES circa 1903

In 1841 a fire broke out in the heating system of one section of the churches. However, the nave and tower were saved. After rebuilding, only three of the four churches were accommodated on the site. By the 1870s the Old Steeple required restoration. It was rebuilt, re-faced and re-opened to the public in 1873. Further external and internal restoration was carried out in the 1960s.

Dundee. *St. Peter's Church*   Valentines Series   23970

Dundee. St. Andrew's Parish Church.

The Wrench Series. No. 9239

LEFT: ST PETER'S CHURCH, PERTH ROAD 1896

This was the first church to be built at the west end of Dundee to cater for the expanding population in that area. It was opened for worship on 15th May 1836 and its first minister was the Rev. Murray McCheyne. Robert Murray McCheyne (1813-1843) was highly regarded and became associated with the religious revival. He became involved with evangelical missions. During his absence on a preaching tour of Aberdeenshire, a typhoid epidemic broke out in Dundee. He returned to the city, visiting the dying and burying the dead. In doing so he caught the disease and after a few days died aged only 29 years old. His body was laid to rest at the south-west corner of the church. The congregation raised money for the McCheyne Memorial Church, Sinderins, which was opened on 12th May 1870.

ABOVE: ST ANDREW'S PARISH CHURCH circa 1904

St Andrew's Parish Church is Dundee's oldest ecclesiastical building which is still intact and is the only Trades Kirk in Scotland. In 1575 the bakers, shoemakers, glovers, tailors, bonnetmakers, fleshers, hammermen, weavers and dyers joined together to form the Nine Incorporated Trades. The masons, wrights and slaters grouped together nearly 200 years later to become the Three United Trades. In the 1760s Dundee's population had expanded. This meant that there was insufficient space for people to worship in the three existing churches in the Nethergate. The tradesmen, at a meeting in the Howff, decided that a fourth church was needed. The kirk session agreed and a public subscription was launched. The trades and kirk Session met the outstanding balance. The church was designed by Samuel Bell in 1772. He had been appointed as Dundee architect in October 1771. The foundation stone was laid in May 1772. The first minister to be appointed as Rev. Thomas Rait, from Scotstown in Tweedsdale, who preached his first sermon on 19th June 1774.

Albert Institute, Dundee   Valentines Series

ABOVE: ALBERT INSTITUTE circa 1898

In 1861 Prince Albert died. Monuments were erected throughout the country to honour his memory. In Dundee a number of notable citizens, which included the Baxters, formed a private company to build a suitable memorial. Dundee Public Library opened in 1869, with books transferred from the Watt Institute, Constitution Road (now the Y.M.C.A.). Dundee Museum and Art Gallery was opened four years later.

TOP RIGHT: ROYAL EXCHANGE, PANMURE STREET circa 1903

Panmure Street, which opened in 1839, was named after Baron Panmure, in recognition of his donations to the Infirmary in 1838. The Royal Exchange, designed by David Bryce of Edinburgh, was opened in 1856. The low building to the left was the Jute Shelter where jute was bought and sold. The statue of Queen Victoria was cast to mark her Diamond Jubilee in 1897.

BOTTOM RIGHT: "COURIER" BUILDING, MEADOWSIDE 1906

The "Courier" Building was designed in 1902. In May 1886 William Thomson, a Dundee shipowner, took over control of the *Dundee Courier* (first published on 20 September 1816) in association with his son, David Couper Thomson. In 1906 they merged with John Leng and Co. Ltd, who published the *Dundee Advertiser* (founded in 1801). In 1926 the *Courier* and the *Advertiser* merged to form one title.

Dundee Weekly News Office,
DUNDEE.

The undernoted Papers have arrived and have been placed at your credit.

Yours truly,

W. & D. C. THOMSON.

190 1

			£	s.	D.
Oct. 22	Copies DUNDEE COURIER, = 48 Doz.			18	
	Copies EVENING POST, = 106 8 Doz.		1	15	4
	Copies WEEKLY NEWS, = 24 6 Doz.		1	.	4½
	Copies WEEKLY WELCOME, = 13 12 Doz.			10	6
	Copies RED LETTER, = 13 Doz.			9	9
			4	14	3½

Please note that this Credit Note must be returned with Remittance. AGENTS are requested to make no alteration on card. Any difference to be noted to Head Office.

ABOVE: INVOICE NOTE *1901*

Postcards were used by businesses. An example is shown above. The *Sunday Post* was first launched in 1914, as the *Post Sunday Special*. A contributor to the success of the paper and to the publisher was the talented and prolific comic artist, Dudley Watkins. He was responsible for drawing "The Broons" and "Oor Wullie" (*Sunday Post*), "Desperate Dan" (*Dandy*) and "Biffo the Bear" (*Beano*).

TOP RIGHT: HER MAJESTY'S THEATRE, SEAGATE *circa 1903*

Early theatrical performances in Dundee were held in the Town House as early as 1755. The first regular theatre in Dundee was at Yeaman Shore and opened on 23 July 1800. This was used until the Theatre Royal in Castle Street, designed by Samuel Bell, was opened on 27 June 1810. The new Theatre Royal opened as Her Majesty's Theatre on 19 October 1885 in the Seagate.

BOTTOM RIGHT: KING'S THEATRE AND HIPPODROME *1912*

The theatre was designed by H. & F. Thompson of Dundee. It was opened by Lady Dunedin of Stenton by laying a memorial stone in the foyer of the theatre on 15 March 1909. The theatre offered performances twice nightly at 7 p.m. and 9 p.m. The King's was converted to a cinema and formally reopened on 24 September 1928 by Lord Provost High. It closed as a cinema in October 1981.

Her Majesty's Theatre, Dundee *I am going here tonight.* Valentines Series

King's Theatre & Hippodrome, Dundee

Dundee.

Court house.

ABOVE: SHERIFF COURT HOUSE, WEST BELL STREET *circa 1904*

For the first 100 years the old Burgh Gaol in the Town House had few occupants. As Dundee's population increased, the number of prisoners increased. By the 1830s a new gaol was required. George Angus submitted a successful design in 1833 for a courthouse, a gaol governor's house, a police office and a gaol.

TOP RIGHT: OLD POST OFFICE *circa 1878*

The headquarters of Dundee Post Office moved about frequently in the 19th century. In 1837 the Dundee Post Office moved to the top of Castle Street. In 1846 larger premises were found at 47 Reform Street. In 1857 the rent for this site increased. The Town Council stepped in and gave the Office a site at the Pillars in the High Street at modest rent. The next move was to Albert Square.

BOTTOM RIGHT: SITE OF NEW GENERAL POST OFFICE *circa 1878*

The Central Post Office, which occupied the site of today's "Courier" building, opened on 23 May 1862. The building, after being used for 36 years, was demolished in December 1898. The GPO building in Meadowside was completed in November 1898. The staff moved everything into the building after completing a day's work, on Saturday 26 November 1898. The New Post Office opened the next morning.

796   *Old Post Office, Dundee*   R. H. Lundie, Reform Street

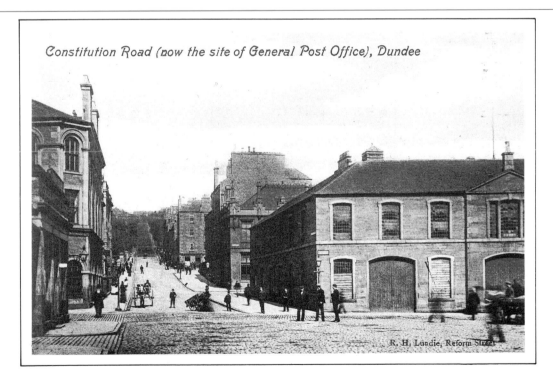

Constitution Road (now the site of General Post Office), Dundee

R. H. Lundie, Reform Street

GENERAL POST OFFICE *1899*
KING'S CROSS HOSPITAL *1903*

Victoria Hospital, Dundee   Valentines Series

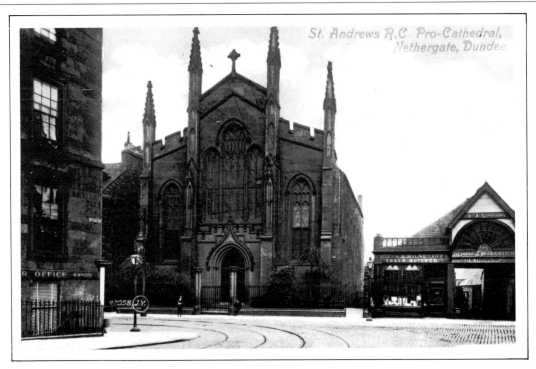

VICTORIA HOSPITAL 1903
ST ANDREW'S R.C. PRO-CATHEDRAL 1905

99

ABOVE: *CALEDONIAN RAILWAY STATION, UNION STREET 1893*
The Dundee and Perth Railway (1847-1863) was formally opened on 22 May 1847 when a train of 30 carriages and three engines travelled along the line from Dundee. In 1866 the line was taken over by the Caledonian Railway. They built the West Station, shown in the picture, in 1890. On 1 May 1963 the last train left the West Station bound for Glasgow.

TOP RIGHT: *CUSTOM HOUSE circa 1904*
The Custom House was opened in 1843. It also served as the headquarters of Dundee Harbour Trust which replaced the Harbour Commission in 1830. The Trust had full control of the harbour and immediately began a programme of dock and wharf construction to cope with the increasing volume of trade. On the left can be seen the old East Station, which was built in 1857.

BOTTOM RIGHT: *ROYAL INFIRMARY circa 1903*
In 1753 a Voluntary Dispensary was organised for the first time in Dundee. On 17 June 1794 the foundation stone for the first Dundee Infirmary was laid in King Street. On 11 March 1798 the first patient was admitted. The old Infirmary had accommodation for 56 patients. On 22 July 1852 the foundation stone for the new Royal Infirmary, Barrack Road, was laid.

Dundee   Custom House.

Royal Infirmary, Dundee

CAIRD HALL, DUNDEE.

ABOVE: CAIRD HALL 1922
Edward Caird (1806-1889), father of Sir James Caird (1837-1916), founded the jute manufacturing firm of Caird (Dundee) Ltd, in 1832. Sir James Caird, who was always considered a good employer, will be remembered as one of the city's main benefactors. He gifted a total of nearly £250,000 between 1895 and his death in 1916. This figure included £100,000 for the Caird Hall.

TOP RIGHT: DOCK STREET AND ROYAL ARCH 1905
The merchants decided in 1807 to build a new Exchange at the foot of Castle Street. In 1830 the new Exchange Coffee Room was opened. In 1856 the Royal Exchange in Panmure Street was built to replace this as the mercantile centre. The "Exchange Coffee House" is now occupied by the publisher David Winter & Sons and is shown to the left of the picture.

BOTTOM RIGHT: GREENMARKET circa 1905
By late Victorian times, the Greenmarket had become the principal market. Scotland's first chip stall was in the Greenmarket. It was run by a Belgian, named Edward de Gernier, who was reputedly the first man to introduce chips to Britain. The Greenmarket remained in existence until 1935 when it was cleared away to make space for the new Shore Terrace Bus Station.

Dock Street and Royal Arch, Dundee

THE GREENMARKET, DUNDEE. LOOKING S.W.

ABOVE: PEOPLE'S PHARMACY, 9 COWGATE 1905

The "People's Pharmacy" was formerly known as the "Edinburgh Pharmacy" under the proprietorship of D. M. Wood. By 1903 the title "People's Pharmacy" had been adopted. Alexander McHardy, shown here with his assistant, took over the shop around 1904. The advertisement displayed in the window is for Wood's Cough Emulsion, "The Reliable Cough Cure". This remedy was sold in bottles for 1s. or 1s. 9d.

TOP RIGHT: JAMES MILLAR'S HAT SHOP circa 1898

The picture shows James T. G. Millar's hat shop at 21 Overgate. In the left window there can be seen a wide variety of cloth caps, bowler hats and top hats. The prices range from half-a-crown to 14s. 6d. In the right window are a selection of shirts, collars and ties. Hanging up in the doorway are a selection of braces. On the right hangs Mrs D. Rosen's pawnbroker sign. In 1900 Dundee had about 25 pawnbrokers.

BOTTOM RIGHT: WILLIAM MILLAR'S GROCERY SHOP, July 1897

William Millar was born in Kirriemuir in 1848. He came to Dundee and joined his cousin, William Lindsay, of Lindsay and Low, where he later became manager. In 1876 he started his own business at 8 Tally Street. As business increased he changed to 38 Nethergate, shown in the picture. In 1898 he moved into larger premises at 75 High Street. He died on 31 August 1913.

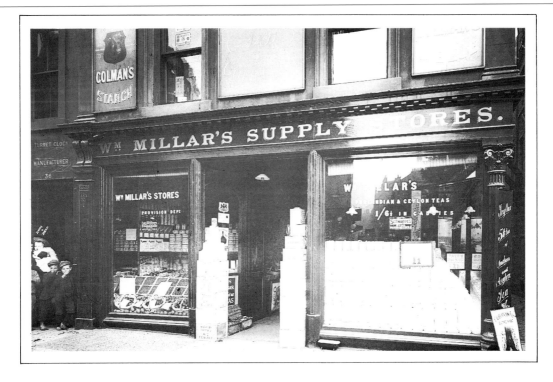

The D. M. Brown Store and Arcade, Dundee

ABOVE: D. M. BROWN STORE AND ARCADE 1908
D. M. Brown's was a large fashionable departmental store. Mr Brown was born in Lochee in 1864. He served his apprenticeship as a draper with Thomas Stewart and Sons, High Street, Lochee. On 31 March 1888 he set up his own business at the corner of High Street and Rankine's Court. The store expanded annually until 1914.

TOP RIGHT: OPENING OF THE ARCADE AT D. M. BROWN'S, 5 July 1906
The first section of the Arcade opened on 5 July 1906. The Arcade provided 80 feet of window space for displaying gowns, coats, children's frocks, white blouses, scarves, millinery and ribbons. This venture proved so successful that in 1908 the Arcade was completed and formed an avenue from High Street to Commercial Street. This card was produced for D. M. Brown by Valentine & Sons Ltd.

BOTTOM RIGHT: THE PILLARED ROOM AT D. M. BROWN'S circa 1920
In 1900 Mr Brown introduced a new feature, by the establishment of tea rooms, on the third floor of the store. He was the first draper in Dundee to adopt this idea. It proved popular and led to other leading drapers copying the concept. The Tea Rooms later developed into Luncheon Rooms.

Opening of the Arcade at D. M. BROWN'S, 80 High Street, Dundee   'Meet me in the Arcade.'

THE PILLARED ROOM AT D. M. BROWN'S, DUNDEE.

ABOVE: TEA ROOMS AT DRAFFEN'S, WHITEHALL STREET circa 1920
The Draffen's business was originally founded in 1833 by William Moon and John Langlands who had a small shop at 10 Overgate. They were the first shopkeepers in Dundee to sell goods by applying fixed prices. Prior to this it was the custom to bargain for purchases. George Draffen and John Jarvie took over the drapery business in 1889.

TOP RIGHT: TAY BRIDGE FROM THE SOUTH 1879
Thomas Bouch (1822-1880) proposed and designed the rail bridge which was built at a cost of £270,000. It took six years to complete and was opened on 31 May 1878. On 28 December 1879, a great storm struck the bridge just as a passenger train was crossing. The bridge collapsed and the train plunged into the Tay at the cost of around 75 lives.

BOTTOM RIGHT: FALLEN GIRDERS, TAY BRIDGE 1879
Bouch's bridge was designed to be constructed of wrought iron girders which rested upon solid masonry piers. However, the soil composition of the river bed was found to be incapable of taking such a load so much lighter cast iron columns were used instead. In addition, poor quality materials were used and poor workmanship was involved. William Barlow (1811-1902) designed the second Tay Bridge.

TAY BRIDGE FROM SOUTH. (AFTER ACCIDENT). 1863. J.V.

Fallen Girders, Tay Bridge

JV 1864

The Engine, Old Tay Bridge Disaster   JV 74707

ABOVE: TAY DISASTER LOCOMOTIVE 1880
The North British Railway Locomotive No. 224 was salvaged from the Tay in April 1880. It took three attempts to recover it because the lifting chains broke twice during the salvage operation. Despite this, damage was superficial. The engine was repaired at Cowlairs, and returned to service where it remained in use until 1917. It later became known as the "Diver".

TOP RIGHT: TAY BRIDGE FROM THE NORTH 1887
Construction of the bridge by the firm of William Arrol of Glasgow provided local employment but the work involved was potentially dangerous. Fourteen men lost their lives over the five-year construction period. At the time this was regarded as a high safety record. On 20 June 1887 passenger services began. The open-air swimming pool shown was opened on 4 August 1879.

BOTTOM RIGHT: QUEEN'S VISIT, 23 August 1907
Queen Alexandra and Princess Victoria set off to Christiana (Oslo) from Craig Pier after a stay at Balmoral. After arriving at Tay Bridge Station they walked across to Craig Pier where they met members of the Harbour Trust. The Queen and Princess then took a seat in the pinnace which conveyed them to the royal yacht. They were followed by a flotilla of small craft.

Tay Bridge from North

Valentines Series

Queen's Visit to Dundee — Her Majesty bids Good-bye to Lord Provost Longair

The Queen's Visit to Dundee, August, 1908

ABOVE: QUEEN'S VISIT, *24 August 1908*

Queen Alexandra and Princess Victoria, after being in residence at Balmoral, departed for Norway via Dundee as they had done the previous year. The Queen was on her way to Christiana to visit her Scandinavian relatives. She was the eldest daughter of King Christian IX of Denmark who had died in 1906. The men in the forefront of the picture were baillies and civic dignitaries.

TOP RIGHT: FLOWER SHOW, *31 August 1905*

The Flower Show was organised annually by the Dundee Horticultural Society. In earlier years the event had been held in Baxter Park, but the move to Magdalen Green enabled larger crowds to visit. The opening of the 45th show was performed by the Countess of Strathmore in white feather boa and black hat. She was accompanied by the Earl of Strathmore and Lady Mary Lyon.

BOTTOM RIGHT: T.S. MARS *circa 1903*

The *Mars*, formerly a battleship, was converted to a training ship in August 1869 and anchored in the Tay. Four hundred boys, aged between 12 and 16, who had come from deprived homes, were placed aboard. On completion of their education many youngsters started a career in the navy. In 1929 the school was closed. The picture shows the "Mars" boys on the railway embankment at Woodhaven.

OPENING OF DUNDEE FLOWER SHOW 31ST AUG 1905.

Mars Training Ship. Dundee R.M.A.

ABOVE: FIRE BRIGADE, BELL STREET circa 1905
The New Central Fire Station, West Bell Street, was opened in 1900. The legendary Captain James S. Weir, shown wearing the epaulettes at the front of the right-hand machine, was appointed Firemaster in 1903 and continued in this position until his death in 1937. He was Dundee's longest-serving Firemaster. In 1903 there were eight permanent staff. A few years later the number increased to 18.

TOP RIGHT: DUNDEE'S NEW MOTOR FIRE PUMP 1911
In the centre of the picture can be seen two steam fire engines. In 1911 Dundee got its first motor fire engine. This underwent a series of tests on 27 December which were witnessed by local Town Councillors. From a depth of six feet the engine could draw water and throw it 159 feet in the air at a rate of 27,000 gallons per hour. The last horses were disposed of by 1917.

BOTTOM RIGHT: FIRE AT WATSON'S BOND, 19 July 1906
The most destructive fire recorded in the history of Dundee took place on Thursday 19 July 1906. It originated in the bonded store of James Watson and Co. Ltd, Distillers, shortly after 6 p.m., when most of the staff had left. The warehouses contained nearly a million gallons of spirits, principally whisky and rum. The fire raged for two days before it was finally quelled.

DUNDEE'S GREATEST FIRE JULY 19 1906

Published at The Post Card Studio, Broughty Ferry.

Scene of the Great Fire at Watson's Bond, Dundee, July 19, 1906.

ABOVE: FIRE AT WATSON'S BOND, *19 July 1906*

The fire spread to nearby buildings, destroying a Co-operative Store; whisky stores belonging to John Robertson & Sons; and a jute warehouse. Other nearby buildings came close to destruction. Fortunately nobody died during the fire but £400,000 worth of damage had been caused in the area. The picture shows the fire after the height of the blaze. On the right lies a hand-drawn hose cart.

TOP RIGHT: ROYAL VISIT, *10 July 1914*

King George V, Queen Mary and Princess Mary visited Dundee and Perth in the summer of 1914. They arrived by train from Edinburgh, at Tay Bridge Station, at 11.30 a.m., where they were met and welcomed by Lord Provost Urquhart (1864-1930). The picture shows the Royal Party as they left the Albert Institute. They proceeded to Ashton Jute Works after a brief stop outside James Keiller & Sons factory in Chapel Street.

BOTTOM RIGHT: ROYAL VISIT, *10 July 1914*

The entrance to Keiller's factory was decorated in the form of an orange grove. The 500 employees present wore white everday uniforms. The women wore linen overalls and Dutch caps whilst the men wore white Eton jackets and chef's caps. Former retired workers sat in front of the stand. Some of the pensioners had worked for nearly 50 years and most with the late Mr Keiller.

Royal Party leaving Albert Institute
Dundee, July 1914.

Royal Visit to Dundee, July 10th 1914
The Crowd at Keiller's Stand.

Royal Progress along Perth Rd. Dundee, July 1914.

ABOVE: ROYAL VISIT, 10 July 1914

The picture shows the procession along Perth Road after visiting Ashton Works. The shops in the background extending from St Peter's Street were: No. 121, David L. Laverock (grocer); No. 119, Mrs David Kermack (confectioner); No. 117, George Pickles (hosiery warehouse); and No. 115, John Williamson (butcher).

TOP RIGHT: ROYAL VISIT, 10 July 1914

The Royal carriage proceeded to Baxter's Dens Works and arrived at a specially laid out entrance at Victoria Road. Lord Provost Urquhart introduced the King and Queen to the chairman and the four directors. The party entered the principal weaving room which had been decorated by the mill girls with bunting and flags. Three hundred girls were engaged at looms operating at high speed.

BOTTOM RIGHT: ROYAL VISIT, 10 July 1914

Outside the weaving room the party met long-serving employees. The oldest worker in the calender was James Wigton, who had spent 56 years with the firm. The picture shows the Royal party leaving Dens Works on Princes Street, heading for Dundee West Station. They left Dundee around 2 p.m. for a visit to Perth, where they opened the new Perth Royal Infirmary.

Royal Progress along Nethergate, Dundee, July 1914.

King and Queen,
leaving Baxter's, Dundee, July 1914.

DUNDEE TANK WEEK. The opening of THE BANK.

ABOVE: *DUNDEE TANK WEEK, 4 February 1918*
Julian the Tank arrived by train from Aberdeen on Sunday, 3 February. On Monday, 4 February, it paraded through town and arrived at Albert Square near the Merchants' Exchange. Citizens were encouraged to enlist and to buy War Savings Certificates. A single tank cost around £5,000. At the end of a week Dundee had raised over £4.5 million.

TOP RIGHT: *ARRIVAL OF A JUTE SHIP FROM CALCUTTA circa 1898*
Many jute ships were built in Dundee. One of the most famous jute clippers was the four-masted *Jutopolis*, launched for Charles Barrie & Co. in 1891. She was built by the Caledon Shipbuilding Co. The jute clipper *Lochee*, built by Alexander Stephen & Sons in Dundee, made the fastest crossing from Calcutta to Dundee in 90 days. Most ships at the time took about 110 days.

BOTTOM RIGHT: *JUTE WAREHOUSE AT THE WHARF circa 1909*
The Crimean War (1854-1856) gave the jute industry a huge boost. Russia was the main source of raw flax. The war endangered supplies. This resulted in a large price increase and extra demand for coarse woven materials. Cox Bros. of Lochee and Gilroy Bros. of Dundee, who had equipped for jute manufacture before the war, were ahead of their competitors, and they never relinquished their lead.

Arrival at Dundee of a Jute Ship from Calcutta

Jute Warehouse at Wharf

DUNDEE

With best wishes from the Jute City.

BALES OF RAW JUTE EN-ROUTE TO THE MILLS.

JAMES WILSON · CONTRACTOR · DUNDEE · N° 24

ABOVE: BALES OF RAW JUTE circa 1908
The jute cart belonged to James Wilson, who was a contractor based in Trades Lane. Pairs of Clydesdale horses were used to pull the heavy lorries laden with bales of jute. Dundee in the 1860s and 1870s was essentially the world jute industry. Throughout the world, jute sacks from Dundee factories carried the world's goods. Jute was also used in mattresses, floorcoverings, ropes and tarpaulins.

TOP RIGHT: COX BROS. LTD, CAMPERDOWN WORKS, LOCHEE 1916
James Cox (1807-1885) started successfully spinning jute in the mid-1820s and founded the family firm in 1841. The American Civil War (1860-1865) brought about expansion to Camperdown Works, which had begun in 1849. The boom years of the 1860s and 1870s were followed by a decline in demand and overcapacity. By 1900 India had captured much of the world jute trade.

BOTTOM RIGHT: COP WINDER circa 1908
The picture shows a cop winder in the spinning department of a Dundee mill. In 1906 average jute workers' wages were 12s. 6d. for a spinner and 13s. 11d. for a weaver. Wages in the textile industry were never high and jute wages were at the lower end of the national scale. The jute industry employed a higher proportion of women than men.

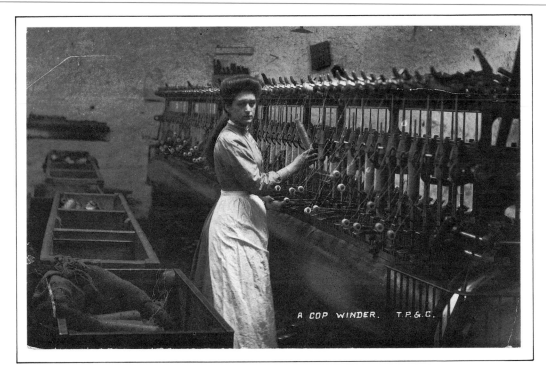

A COP WINDER. T.P.&C.

ABOVE: WEAVERS *circa 1911*

The picture shows weavers at T. L. Miller and Co., Hillside Works. Weavers were traditionally regarded as skilled and well paid compared to spinners. The workers in the picture all look exhausted. They often felt a sickness from the smell of oil and dust, but they dare not complain. The women, tied to one machine, overcame isolation by sign language which evolved against the roar of noisy machinery.

TOP RIGHT: FLOUR MILLS, *4 May 1909*

The foundation and development of Dundee Flour Mills was due to Dr John F. White (1830-1904) and his assistant W. G. Anderson. Dr White took over his father's flourishing milling business in Aberdeen and started Dundee Flour Mills in 1876. In 1888 Dr White closed down the Aberdeen mill and transferred his headquarters to Dundee. Dr White died in October 1904.

BOTTOM RIGHT: LOCOMOTIVE "EARL OF AIRLIE" *circa 1865*

The Dundee and Newtyle Railway (1831-1846) started operating a limited service between Dundee Law and Hatton Hill, near Newtyle, on 6 December 1831. Horses initially hauled carriages along the two level sections of the route. These were replaced in 1833 by locomotives *Earl of Airlie* and *Lord Wharncliffe*, purchased from J. & C. Carmichael of Dundee at a cost of £700 each.

Dundee Flour Mills May 4th 1909.

SELECT BIBLIOGRAPHY

Adamson, P. and Lamont-Brown, R., *Victorian and Edwardian Dundee and Broughty Ferry* (Alvie Publications, 1981)

Brindle, G. D., *Harris Academy: The First 100 Years* (Taurus Print, 1985)

Brotchie, A. W., *Tramways of the Tay Valley* (Dundee Museums and Art Galleries, 1965)

Brotchie, A. W. and Herd, J. J., *North Fife from Old Photographs* (N.B. Traction Group, 1982)

Brotchie, A. W. and Herd, J. J., *Old Dundee from the Tram Cars* (N.B. Traction Group, 1974)

Brotchie, A. W. and Herd, J. J., *Old Dundee: Closes and other Corners* (N.B. Traction Group, 1979)

Byatt, A., *Picture Postcards and their Publishers* (Golden Age Postcard Books, 1978)

Cain, A. M., *Scots in India: The Cornchest for Scotland* (National Library for Scotland, Edinburgh, 1986)

Davey, N., *Dundee By Gaslight* (Dundee Museums and Art Galleries, 1975)

Dundee Social Union Report on Housing and Industrial Conditions in Dundee (John Leng & Co. Ltd, Dundee, 1905)

Dundee Year Books (John Leng & Co. Ltd, Dundee, 1870-1916)

Flood, T., *The Mills Observatory: A Historical Survey* (Dundee Museums and Art Galleries, 1986)

Hartwich, V. C., *Ale an' A'thing: Aspects of the Grocery and Licensed Trades in Dundee 1800-1950* (Dundee Museums and Art Galleries, 1980)

Hill, C. W., *Discovering Picture Postcards* (Shire Publications, 1970)

Kennedy, R. D., *"Dundee Newspapers", 150 Proud Years of the School in Euclid Crescent* (1984)

Lenman, B., Lythe, C. and Gauldie, E., *Dundee and its Textile Industry 1850-1914* (Abertay Historical Society, 1969)

Mair, J., "A Family Empire", *Scots Magazine* (D. C. Thomson, August 1983)

McKean, C. and Walker, D., *Dundee: An Illustrated Introduction* (R.I.A.S/Scottish Academic Press, 1984)

Millar, A. H., *Glimpses of Old and New Dundee* (MacLeod, 1925)

Millar, A. H., *Haunted Dundee* (MacLeod, 1923)

Perkins, J., *Steam Trains to Dundee 1831-1863* (Dundee Museums and Art Galleries, 1975)

Phillips, D., *Pictorial Dundee No. 1* (Winter, 1977)

Shafe, M., *University Education in Dundee 1881-1981: A Pictorial History* (University of Dundee, 1982)

Sidey, T., *"Simple, bold and effective": An Architectural History of The Albert Institute, Dundee* (Dundee Museum and Art Galleries, 1978)

Sidey, T., *Valentines of Dundee* (Dundee Museums and Art Galleries, 1979)

Smout, T. C., *A Century of the Scottish People 1830-1950* (Fontana, 1986)

Taylor, S., "The Trades Kirk", *Scots Magazine* (D. C. Thomson, November 1982)

Thompson, J. H. and Ritchie, G. G., *Dundee Harbour Trust Centenary 1830-1930, History and Development of the Harbour of Dundee* (Dundee Harbour Trust, 1930)

Walker, D. M., *Dundee Architecture and Architects 1770-1914* (Abertay Historical Society, 1977)